For Basil, Uncle Peter, and my parents

CROCODILE'S TEARS

Alex Beard

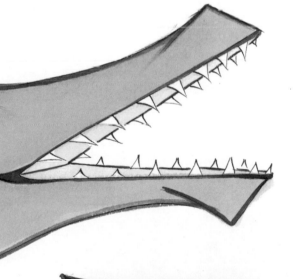

Abrams Books for Young Readers, London

On the banks of the Mburu River in Africa, Crocodile lay in the sun.

He opened his eyes and began to cry.

Rhino and Tickbird came down to the river to drink.

Rhino asked, "Why is Crocodile crying?"

Tickbird squawked, "I don't know, and crocodiles are dangerous, so I wouldn't ask. If we can find a wise golden eagle, you could ask him.

Golden eagles fly much higher, and see much farther than I can. They are very rare, but if anyone would know why Crocodile is crying, he might."

Rhino and Tickbird set off to find a golden eagle. They walked to the steep cliffs of Mount Kivoi and searched the crags and crevices for a nest.

They looked high and low, but found no sign, until at long last they spotted a lone eagle perched on a tall peak. Rhino asked him, "Do you know why Crocodile is crying?"

Golden Eagle called, "It's a bad idea to ask a crocodile anything, so I wouldn't know. Maybe he misses the elephants.

I used to watch huge herds of big tuskers march across the plains, but their trumpets rarely sound anymore. If you can find an elephant, you could ask him."

Rhino and Tickbird went in search of an elephant. They found no tracks. Until, at the end of the day, they heard the stomping footsteps of an immense old bull.

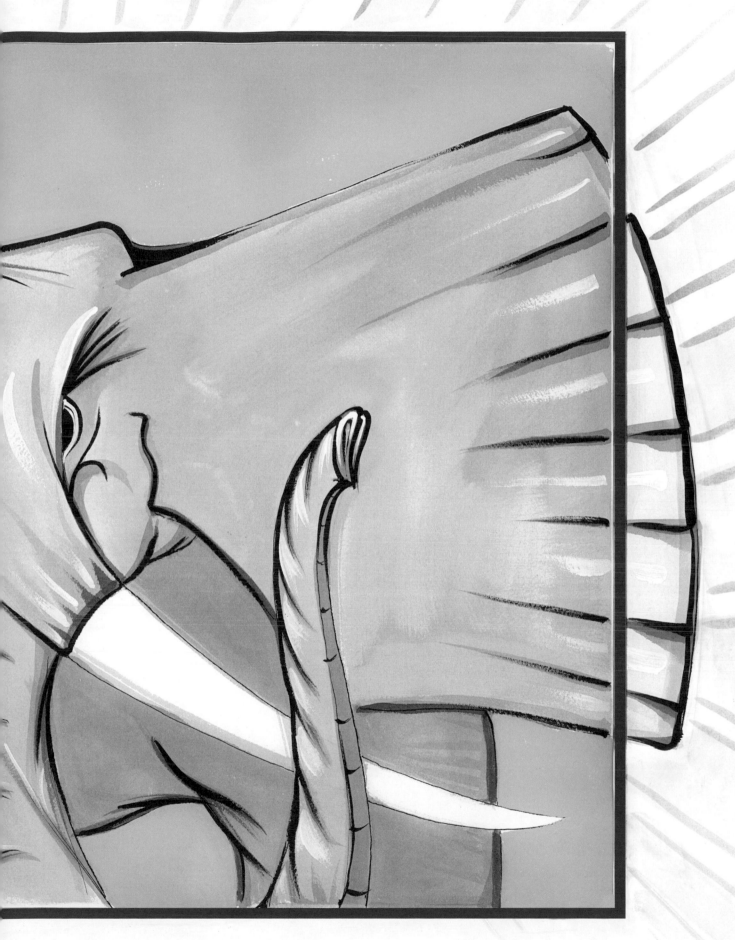

Rhino asked him, "Do you know why Crocodile is crying? Golden Eagle thinks it's because he misses your trumpeting herds."

Elephant harrumphed. "I try not to get near crocodiles, so I don't know. If he's crying for memorable sounds, he could be longing for the song of the tree frogs.

I used to go to the forest after the sun went down to listen to the tree frogs singing, but lately it's been very quiet. If you can find a tree frog, you could ask him."

That evening, Rhino and Tickbird went to the forest, and though they strained to listen, they didn't hear a peep.

Until, just before dawn, they heard the solo crooning of a long-toed tree frog. Rhino asked him, "Do you know why Crocodile is crying? Elephant said it was for your beautiful singing."

Tree Frog croaked, "I would never ask Crocodile myself, so I couldn't know. If he is crying for beautiful things, maybe he misses the butterflies.

Butterflies decorated with dazzling patterns used to flit through the meadow, but they've mostly disappeared. If you can find a butterfly, you could ask him."

Rhino and Tickbird stood in the meadow at the edge of the forest all the next morning. The breeze brought no butterflies until just past noon.

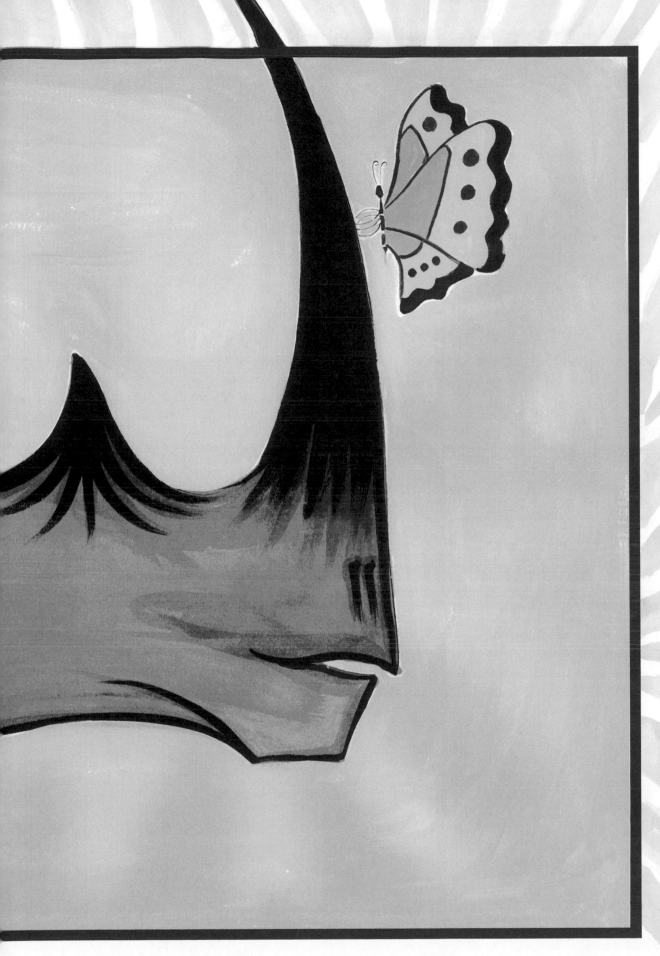

A brilliant Brenton Blue wafted onto Rhino's horn. Rhino asked him, "Do you know why Crocodile is crying? Tree Frog said it was for the lovely patterns in your wings."

Butterfly fluttered with Tree Frog's compliment, but said, "I try to stay away from crocodiles, so I wouldn't know. If it's for something lovely, perhaps he misses the silhouettes of giraffes on the horizon.

Giraffes used to live all across the savanna. They were so graceful it looked like they were walking in slow motion. It's a rare sight now, but if you can find a giraffe, you could ask him."

Rhino and Tickbird crossed the savanna. They made it all the way to the edge of the Great Mwengi Desert before they found a Maasai giraffe.

Rhino asked him, "Do you know why Crocodile is crying? Butterfly says it could be for your graceful silhouette."

Giraffe snorted. "I know better than to get close to a crocodile, so I wouldn't know. If he's crying for graceful things, perhaps he misses the cheetah's sprint.

Cheetahs used to race across the grasslands as quick as lightning, but they're scarce now. If you can find a cheetah, you could ask him."

Rhino and Tickbird headed to the grasslands.
All that night, they looked for the lithe, quick cat.
They found Cheetah, just before his morning hunt.

Rhino asked him, "Do you know why Crocodile is crying? Giraffe says it's because he misses your speed."

Cheetah growled. "I wouldn't ask a crocodile myself, but there's nothing wrong with my sprinting, only where I can go to do it. If Crocodile is crying, it's probably for the vast open spaces.

The illustrations in this book were made with pen and ink and watercolor on paper.

ISBN 978-1-4197-0126-9

Book design by Chad W. Beckerman

Printed and bound in China
10 9 8 7 6 5 4 3 2 1

ABRAMS
THE ART OF BOOKS SINCE 1949
72-82 Rosebery Avenue
London, UK EC1R 4RW
www.abramsbooks.co.uk

TREE FROG (Long-Toed Tree Frog): Although the long-toed tree frog doesn't exactly "sing," it does have a rhythmic voice, producing two brief croaks separated by long intervals. But that voice is heard less and less in Africa, as the species is endangered and the population is on the decline. The frog can be found only in a small range in southern Africa, and it is threatened by fires, the spread of new plants that dry out its habitat, and the growth of the human population.

BRENTON BLUE BUTTERFLY: Although the Brenton Blue butterfly is not completely blue, there are traces of blue on its beautifully patterned wings. Unfortunately, the species is critically endangered, and the only known colony is on the Brenton Blue Butterfly Reserve in Knysna, South Africa. Because the population is so small, the species could be easily wiped out by chance events, such as drought or fire. Therefore, the reserve must be carefully monitored and managed.

MAASAI GIRAFFE: Their long necks and graceful stature make it easy for Maasai giraffes to see all of their surroundings on the African savanna. But today those surroundings are shrinking, as the human population is destroying their habitat. Poaching is another major threat to the species; their beautiful coats can be very valuable. Although they are considered to be at lower risk for endangerment, the population is on the decline.

CHEETAH: The cheetah is the world's fastest land animal—it can sprint up to seventy miles per hour! Unfortunately, there is less and less land for them to run across. Shrinking habitat, loss of species of prey, and hunting have left the species very vulnerable to endangerment. Some African countries have developed conservation strategies for cheetahs, but given their need for large areas, any significant conservation efforts require major, landscape-scale action.

OSTRICH: Contrary to popular belief, ostriches do not actually bury their heads in the sand or earth. To hide from predators, they do stretch out and lay their heads and necks flat on the ground, making them appear as though they are simply a mound of earth. Although they are not yet endangered, their population is on the decline.

GLOSSARY OF ANIMALS

CROCODILE: Crocodiles really do produce tears to keep their eyes from drying out in the sun. But Crocodile also has real reasons to be sad. From the 1940s to the 1960s, African crocodiles were hunted, primarily for their skins, and the population was severely depleted. Thankfully, national laws and international trade regulations saved the species from extinction. But today, the wetlands in which they live are being destroyed by pollution and human developments. Crocodiles are considered a "lower-risk" species for endangerment, but their situation could worsen if human population and hunting trends are not kept in check.

BLACK RHINOCEROS: The black rhinoceros species is critically endangered. Because of relentless hunting and destruction of land for settlement and agricultural purposes, the black rhinoceros population has declined by more than ninety percent over the past sixty years. Although the population is beginning to increase again thanks to conservation programs and better law enforcement, there is still much work to be done to protect the species.

TICKBIRD (Yellow-Billed Oxpecker): The tickbird, or yellow-billed oxpecker, eats insects and ticks, which it finds on large mammals like rhinoceroses and buffalo. That's why Tickbird is always with Rhino. During the 1920s, the tickbird was considered practically extinct in South Africa as a result of the overhunting of its host animals. The species has since bounced back, but today the population is once again on the decline due to big game hunting and destruction of land.

GOLDEN EAGLE: While the golden eagle used to live in the plains and forests of Africa, today the bird is largely a mountain-dweller because of the destruction of its habitat. This destruction has also led to a scarcity of its prey—mice, foxes, and goats, among other animals—making survival more difficult. Although the golden eagle is not considered an endangered species because of its large Asian and American populations, the African population has become very small. Today the golden eagle is only found scattered sparsely throughout northern Africa.

ELEPHANT: Elephants live throughout Africa, but in much smaller numbers than in centuries past. The major cause for their decline is the loss of their habitat due to human population expansion. Another major threat is poaching—the illegal hunting of elephants for their ivory tusks and meat. Efforts have been made to increase legal protection and conservation efforts, but the population still does not enjoy the numbers and freedom it once did.

Rift Valley, at the base of the Loita Hills in Kenya. Some of the animals in this book—such as giraffes, elephants, and the occasional cheetah—live within the preserve. The Trust ensures that the animals there will continue to have a corner of the world in which to live, and I thank you for your contribution to that end.

Finally, I would like to say, "Don't be an ostrich!" Do something, no matter how small, to help protect the environment. Don't use plastic bags. Recycle. Compost for your garden. Make sure your family drives a fuel-efficient car and be mindful of the consequences of wastefulness. Every little bit matters. Together, we can make sure that Crocodile doesn't have to shed any more unnecessary tears.

And Rhino and Tickbird were left in peace to pursue an answer to their next big question: "Why is Hyena laughing?"

AUTHOR'S NOTE

Alex Beard with a Maasai guide at Shompole.

Crocodiles are among the longest-living species on the planet. Through their generations, they have been witness to the extinction of everything from the dinosaurs to the woolly mammoth and the dodo bird. They have seen the expansion and melting of the ice ages and the emergence of man. Therefore, I thought it appropriate for a crocodile, whose ancestors have seen so many species come and go over the millions of years of their existence, to be the mechanism through which this book could explore the current extinction crisis. Crocodile weeps "crocodile tears" for the ongoing collapse of the wild and its inhabitants.

While not all the animals in this book are critically endangered, some are, and moreover, the environment in which they all live is under siege. In this book, I include animals that usually live in diverse settings across a wide range of terrain in close enough proximity to one another to give Rhino and Tickbird the opportunity to visit them. The locales are set according to the fictional geography utilized in my first two books, *The Jungle Grapevine* and *Monkey See, Monkey Draw*.

I love nature and have visited parts of Africa and other "wild" places on this planet through the years. I have witnessed firsthand that we humans as a species are on the verge of irrevocably damaging our fragile world. To help preserve the animals I love and the environment in which they live, I am donating a portion of the proceeds from the sale of this book to the Shompole Community Trust. Shompole, an example of a successful preservation effort jointly overseen by the Maasai people and the Shompole Camp, is located on the western escarpment of the Great

However, because crocodile is Green, it didn't sit well with him to eat a black rhino. He spat him back out.

Crocodile ate him all up.

But, since you asked, Black Rhino, it could be because I'm going to miss you." And with that, Crocodile did another thing that crocodiles do.

Crocodile smiled. "I'm crying because it is hot in the sun, and the tears keep my eyes moist and healthy. It's one of the things crocodiles do.

In spite of Tickbird's warnings, Rhino returned to where Crocodile still lay weeping on the banks of the river. He asked him, "Why are you crying?"

Rhino thought about all the possible reasons for Crocodile's tears. He knew that any of them were worthy, but he wanted to know the truth.

And he definitely didn't want to think about why Crocodile might be crying. Ostrich buried his head in the sand.

This was too much for Ostrich. He didn't want to think about eagles and elephants, or tree frogs and butterflies, or cheetahs and the open spaces where they once lived.

Rhino and Tickbird were at a loss. They couldn't ask the land itself why Crocodile was crying. So when Ostrich wandered by, they asked him.

Rhino said, "Do you know why Crocodile is crying? Does he miss the soaring eagles or the trumpeting elephant herds? Does he long for the singing of the tree frogs, the beauty of the butterflies' wings, and the grace of the giraffes' silhouettes? Or is he crying for the land where the cheetahs used to run free?"

Cheetahs used to run in all directions as fast as we could. But there are very few places left to really stretch our legs. Roads and fences have sprung up everywhere to block our path."